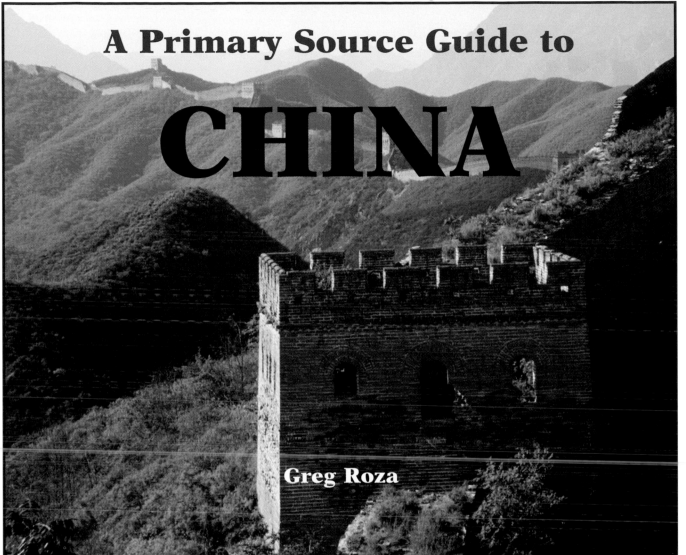

A Primary Source Guide to
CHINA

Greg Roza

The Rosen Publishing Group's

PowerKids Press™
PRIMARY SOURCE

New York

Published in 2003 by The Rosen Publishing Group, Inc.
29 East 21st Street, New York, NY 10010

Book Design: Haley Wilson

Photo Credits: Cover, p. 1 © The Image Bank; p. 4 © Dallas & John Heaton/Corbis; p. 6 © Map Resources; p. 6 (inset) © Keren Su/Corbis; p. 8 (oracle bone) © Royal Ontario Museum/Corbis; pp. 8 (inset), 20 © Lowell Georgia/Corbis; p. 10 © Roger Ressmeyer/Corbis; p. 11 © Bettmann/Corbis; p. 12 © Charles & Josette Lenars/Corbis; p. 14 © Yann Layma/Stone; p. 15 © Bruce Ayres/Stone; p. 16 © Paul A. Souders/Corbis; p. 17 © Jack Fields/Corbis; p. 18 © Carl & Ann Purcell/Corbis; p. 19 © Burstein Collection/Corbis; p. 22 © Eyewire.

Library of Congress Cataloging-in-Publication Data

Roza, Greg.
  A primary source guide to China / Greg Roza.
      p. cm.
Includes index.
Summary: Text and photographs depict the history, government, culture, and traditions of China, which shares its borders with fourteen other countries.
  ISBN 0-8239-6591-0 (library binding)
  ISBN 0-8239-8075-8 (pbk.)
  6-pack ISBN: 0-8239-8082-0
  1. China—Juvenile literature. [1. China.] I. Title.
  DS706 .R84 2003
  951—dc21
                                    2002004164

Manufactured in the United States of America

Contents

Home of the Great Wall   5

The Land of China   7

Dynasties   9

Chinese Government   11

The Economy   13

The People of China   15

Beliefs and Customs   17

The History of Art in China   19

China Today   21

China at a Glance   22

Glossary   23

Index   24

Primary Source List   24

Web Sites   24

Home of the Great Wall

China is a country in southeast Asia. To the east of China is the Pacific Ocean. China shares its borders with fourteen countries, including Russia, India, and Mongolia. Shanghai is the largest city in China. Beijing is the capital and second largest city in China.

You have probably heard of the Great Wall of China. It is more than 2,000 years old! Early Chinese societies built the wall to guard their land from their enemies to the north.

◄ The Great Wall of China is the largest man-made structure in the world. It is about 4,500 miles (7,242 kilometers) long! This photograph shows part of the wall near Beijing.

KAZAKSTAN

RUSSIA

MONGOLIA

GOBI DESERT

Beijing★

CHINA

NORTH KOREA

SO KO

Yellow Sea

HIMALAYAS

Yangtze

NEPAL

East C Se

INDIA

Yangtze River

Shanghai

Taipei

TAIWAN

6

VIETNAM

Hong Kong

LAOS

THAILAND

South China Sea

The Land of China

China is the third largest country in the world. Only Russia and Canada are bigger. Most Chinese people live in the eastern part of the country because the land there is good for farming. This is also where most of China's large cities are.

Not many people live in the western part of China because the land is not good for farming. The tallest mountain range in the world—the Himalaya mountains—stretches across southwestern China. The Gobi Desert covers a large part of northern China.

◀ China has one of the longest rivers in the world, the Yangtze. The Yangtze is more than 3,900 miles (6,276 kilometers) long! It starts in China's western mountains and flows into the East China Sea near the city of Shanghai.

Chinese coins

8

Dynasties

Throughout its history, China has been ruled by many powerful **dynasties**. The first dynasty was the Xia (SHE-AH) Dynasty. It lasted from about 2100 B.C. to 1800 B.C. The next dynasty—the Shang Dynasty—was the first to keep written records.

Over the next 1,600 years, different societies fought each other for control of China. In 221 B.C., the Qin (CHIN) Dynasty came to power. The leaders of the Qin Dynasty created systems of writing, money, and measurements. They rebuilt and connected many old walls to form the Great Wall of China.

◀ Scientists have found thousands of shells and bones with early Chinese writing on them. These are called "oracle bones." They show some of the earliest forms of writing in the world. Some are thousands of years old! The small picture shows Chinese coins that are almost 2,000 years old.

Chinese Government

Beginning with the Qin Dynasty, China was ruled by emperors. Emperors had to struggle to control their territories because people were spread out over large areas of land. Enemies from the north often tried to take land from the emperors and their people.

Today, China is one of the only **Communist** countries in the world. In a Communist country, the government owns most of the large businesses. It also owns and runs many services, such as banks and airlines. The people do not have a say in how the government and large businesses are run.

战无不胜的毛泽东思想万岁！

LONG LIVE THE INVINCIBLE
THOUGHT OF MAO TSE-TUNG!

▲ This sign praising Mao Tsc-Tung is at the entrance of a hotel in China.

◀ Mao Tse-Tung, also called Mao Zedong, was China's first Communist leader. He led a revolt against rich landowners in the early 1900s and ruled China's Communist Party until his death in 1976. This portrait was painted in 1989.

The Economy

More than half of China's workers are farmers. China is a leading producer of cotton, rice, tea, and wheat. China trades many of these products to other countries in return for metals and machines, which are needed to build and run China's factories.

Manufacturing has become important to China's **economy** since the rise of Communism. China's leaders have struggled to change their country from a farming nation to a manufacturing nation to compete with other countries.

Chinese money is called "yuan." This yuan is decorated with a picture of the Great Wall of China.

China has the world's largest fishing industry. Many people make their living by fishing. China is also a world leader in the mining of iron, gold, and lead.

13

The People of China

Almost 1.3 billion people live in China today. That's about one-fifth of the world's population!

In the past, family and public rules in China were very strict. Today, they are not as strict, but manners are still very important in modern Chinese society. Chinese people believe it is important to show respect to their elders. Chinese **customs** from the past are also still important today. For example, giving gifts during special events is a way to show respect for others.

Great care is taken in naming Chinese children. Many Chinese people believe that a baby's name can decide the child's future. Family is very important in China. The above photograph shows four generations of a Chinese family.

16

Beliefs and Customs

Many Chinese beliefs and customs were shaped by the teachings of a man named Confucius, who  lived about 2,500 years ago. Confucius taught that we should honor the past, treat each other with kindness, and always try to do the right thing. Some people consider his teachings a religion.

statue of Confucius

The most important **celebration** in China is the Spring Festival, or Chinese New Year. Chinese families honor their **ancestors** and celebrate the new year. Children receive red envelopes filled with "lucky money" to bring good fortune in the coming year.

◀ Chinese people celebrate Chinese New Year by performing dragon and lion dances. They also light firecrackers to chase away evil spirits.

The History of Art in China

Painting, **sculpture**, and pottery have been popular art forms in China for thousands of years. China also has a long musical history. More than 2,000 years ago, the Chinese had already created many musical instruments, such as drums and stringed instruments. Chinese operas, first performed about 700 years ago, are still popular today.

Some works of Chinese writing are more than 3,000 years old. Chinese writing itself has long been considered a form of art. Artistic Chinese writing is called **calligraphy**.

◀ This painting, which has calligraphy in the upper right corner, was done about 300 years ago.

◀ China has some of the world's oldest works of art. These statues of Chinese soldiers are more than 2,000 years old. They were found in the tomb of China's first emperor, Shi Huang Di, near the city of Xian.

China Today

Communists took control of China in 1949. The people who had been in control before 1949 moved to the nearby island of Taiwan. The **United Nations** recognized Taipei, a city in Taiwan, as China's capital until 1971. Since then, the United Nations has recognized Beijing as the capital. Relations between the "two Chinas" are still tense.

Chinese **culture** continues to grow in spite of China's stormy political history. Like the Great Wall, China's people have survived the test of time. Its leaders believe that educating their children will help the country reach its political and economic goals.

◀ Chinese children start school when they are about six years old. They study history, science, and math, just like students in the United States do. They also study the Chinese language, arts, and politics.

China at a Glance

Population: About 1.3 billion

Capital City: Beijing (population about 7,500,000)

Largest City: Shanghai (population about 9,000,000)

Official Name: People's Republic of China

National Anthem: "March of the Volunteers"

Land Area: 3,705,822 square miles (9,598,035 square kilometers)

Government: Communist

Government Leader: Premier

Unit of Money: Yuan

Flag: The large star on the flag stands for leaders of the Communist Party. The four little stars stand for groups of workers.

Glossary

ancestor (AN-ses-tuhr) A family member who lived before you.

calligraphy (kuh-LIH-gruh-fee) The art of beautiful writing.

celebration (seh-luh-BRAY-shun) A special event honoring something important.

Communist (KAH-myoo-nist) A system of government in which almost everything is owned and run by the state.

culture (KUL-chur) The beliefs, art, religions, and ways of life of a group of people.

custom (KUH-stuhm) The accepted way of doing something that is passed down within a group of people.

dynasty (DIE-nuh-stee) A line of rulers who belong to the same family.

economy (ee-KAH-nuh-mee) The way a country or business uses its money and goods.

sculpture (SKULP-chur) A form made out of clay, rock, wood, or metal.

United Nations (yoo-NIE-ted NAY-shunz) A worldwide group formed at the end of World War II to keep peace between nations of the world.

Index

A
Asia, 5

B
Beijing, 5, 21, 22

C
calligraphy, 19
Chinese New Year, 17
Communist(s), 11, 21, 22
Confucius, 17

F
farming, 7, 13

G
Gobi Desert, 7
Great Wall, 5, 9, 21

H
Himalaya mountains, 7

M
manufacturing, 13

Q
Qin Dynasty, 9, 11

S
Shang Dynasty, 9
Shanghai, 5, 22

T
Taipei, 21
Taiwan, 21

U
United Nations, 21

X
Xia Dynasty, 9

Primary Source List

Page 4. Great Wall. The Qin Dynasty (221 B.C.–207 B.C.) built the first Great Wall by joining short walls that had been built earlier. Most of the wall we see today is a wall built during the Ming Dynasty (1368–1644).

Page 8 (large image). Oracle bone. During the Shang Dynasty (1766 B.C.–1050 B.C.), ox bones were thrown into fire to find the gods' answers to questions. The pattern of cracks caused by the fire revealed the answers, which were then written on the bone. This oracle bone is in the Royal Ontario Museum in Toronto, Canada.

Page 8 (inset). Old Chinese coins. Early writing appears on these Chinese bronze coins, which date to around the time of the Qin Dynasty. They are in the Luoyang Municipal Museum, Luoyang, Henan, China.

Page 10. Portrait of Mao Zedong. The 20-foot-high portrait of Mao hangs above the Gate of Heavenly Peace outside the Imperial Palace in Beijing. From 1972 to 1999, the immense portraits were painted by an artist named Wang Qizhi. He had to replace the portrait twice a year because of damage from sunlight and smog.

Page 11. Billboard, entrance to Eastwind Hotel, Guangzhou (Canton), China.

Page 13. 1-yuan banknote. Issued in 1996.

Page 17. Statue of Confucius, Dacheng Hall, Confucius Temple, Qufu, China. Qufu is the birthplace of Confucius. Original temple built in 478 B.C. Dacheng Hall built ca. 1725.

Page 18. Statues of soldiers from first emperor's tomb. When Shi Huang Di died in 210 B.C., he was buried in this tomb in Xian, along with 7,000 life-size terra-cotta statues of soldiers to guard him. The tomb also contained weapons and statues of horses. Peasants digging a well discovered the tomb in 1974.

Page 19. Landscape painting. Qing Dynasty painter Tao Chi (1641–1710) painted this view of a house in the mountains sometime between 1662 and 1710. It comes from his *Album of Twelve Landscape Paintings*.

Web Sites

Due to the changing nature of Internet links, The Rosen Publishing Group, Inc. has developed an on-line list of Web sites related to the subjects of this book. This site is updated regularly. Please use this link to access the list:
http://www.powerkidslinks.com/pswc/psch/

DUE